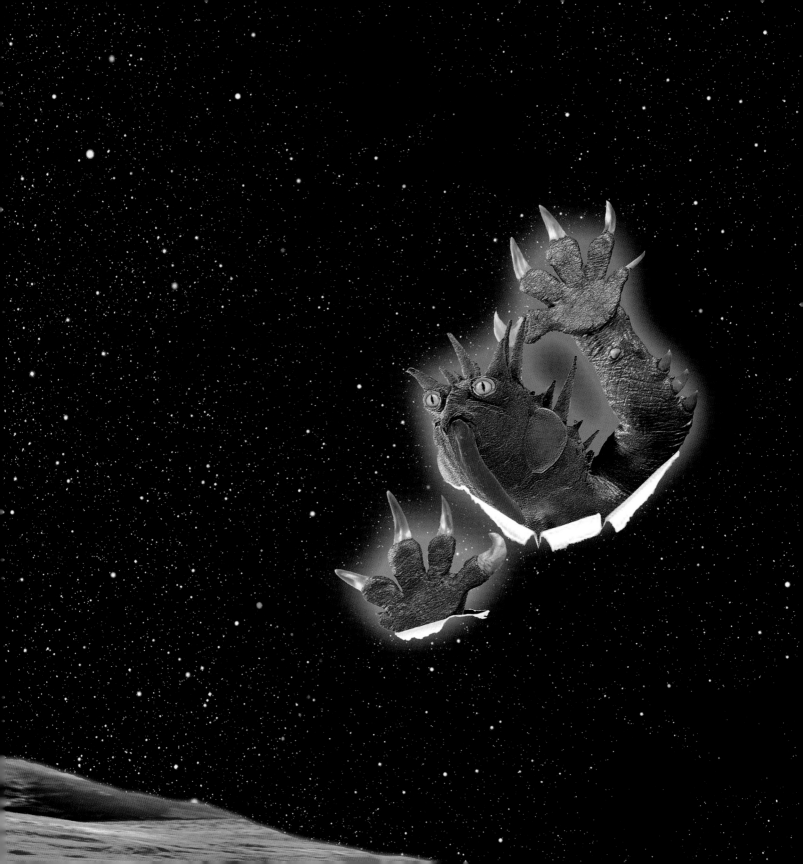

EN
DS

LIFE   BY DAVID A. AGUILAR

NATIONAL GEOGRAPHIC
WASHINGTON, D.C.

CONTENTS

YOUR ALIEN WORLDS ITINERARY

In these pages, you will travel to eight planets (including a rare double world!) specially created for this book on your journey to find alien life. Each planet you visit is modeled on an actual type of planet scientists have discovered in the Milky Way galaxy. The aliens are imagined creatures based on scientific realities about how life forms in different environments. We can look at factors such as gravity, temperature, and availability of light and water to determine what form each planet's inhabitants might take. Someday we may have the means to travel to these distant worlds, so we can meet any possible inhabitants ourselves. For now, we use scientifically based speculation to imagine all the exciting possibilities of life beyond Earth.

—DA

INTRODUCTION

ALIEN SPACE SCOUTS WANTED!
Your mission awaits. You are needed out there in the galaxy—our own Milky Way, our illustrious city of stars—pronto!

THE BACKGROUND
First, look at the array of aliens we see here. Are they nothing more than figments of a vast and wild imagination? Could Earthbound humans really be the only intelligent beings in our universe? Or, if we apply our knowledge of biology, botany, chemistry, and evolution to newly discovered alien worlds circling distant stars, would we encounter something wondrously different?

THE MISSION
Now is the time to use your science-based imagination to help investigate eight exoplanets, planets existing "exo," or outside, our own solar system. This book is your guide to detecting, observing, and analyzing strange new life-forms on distant worlds. We are about to take the wildest space safari ever.

SOME WORDS OF CAUTION
Do not try to feed these life-forms. They are not like any other creatures you have seen before and may have a few surprises you might not find so pleasant.

Twenty-first-century explorers, we want this mission to be a big success. Anticipate some serious alien finds, explore well, and come home in one piece. *Alien Space Scouts, it's time to say goodbye to our solar system and travel to the stars. Are you ready?*

SO MANY STARS, SO MANY POSSIBILITIES!

Check this out. The Milky Way is the galaxy we call our home. There are 200 billion stars and at least 230 million Earth-like planets in it. Look closer. See all those white smudges surrounding our galaxy? Each one is another galaxy made of billions of stars with trillions of planets circling around them. There are more galaxies in the universe than all the snowflakes that have ever fallen on Earth. That should make your head spin!

With all these stars and planets out there, the challenge is trying to figure out which ones would be the best for life. Knowing that our planet supports intelligent life, we begin our search by looking for alien planets similar to Earth. But how do we go about finding them?

BEST STARS FOR LIFE

First, forget the big, hot O, B, and A stars. Like big gas-guzzling cars, they burn through their hydrogen fuel too quickly to support life. In just a few hundred million years, they blow up or turn into black holes. No time for life to get started here. Medium-size F and G stars, like our sun, and smaller K stars are much better choices. They shine for billions of years. Tiny M stars burn for trillions of years.

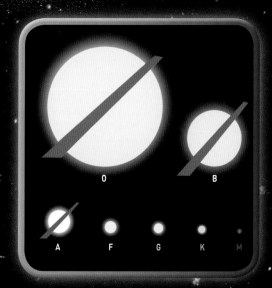

O B A F G K M

HOW PLANETS FORM

Planets are a natural part of star formation. As huge clouds of gas and dust swirl together like cosmic hurricanes, planets form out of the leftovers orbiting the star. Like our own solar system, closer-in planets tend to be smaller and made out of iron, rock, and water. Planets like Neptune and Jupiter, forming farther away from their star, are larger and made out of ice and gas. When searching for Earth-like planets, it is the smaller rocky ones that we are focused on.

HABITABLE ZONES OF STARS

One of the critical components for life is water. The best place to find planets with oceans and lakes is in an area called the habitable zone. This is the distance from a star where water can exist as a liquid. Think of a star as a campfire. The bigger and hotter the fire, the farther away you want to be, or you get way too hot. With a smaller, cooler fire, you move closer in to stay warm. Like you with the fire, that just-right space away from a star makes planets an ideal temperature for water, and so also for life. The distances separating stars and the planets in their habitable zones also determine how long it takes the planet to orbit around the star. Located 93 million miles (150 million km) from the sun, it takes Earth 365.25 days to complete one orbit. But Earth-like planets orbiting smaller stars may take just a few months to complete one orbit. Think of how many more birthdays you could celebrate on worlds like that!

HOW WE IDENTIFY ALIEN PLANETS

I n the movies it's easy! The aliens always come to us. Arriving in big ugly spaceships, the first thing they usually do is start blasting away at our cities. Don't they have anything better to do? Luckily for us, no real alien invaders have come to vacation here yet. So, if we really want to know if aliens exist out there, how do we find them?

WOBBLY STARS

Our first success in finding possible alien planets came using instruments that measured how much distant stars wobbled in space. When planets circle their stars, they pull on them, causing the star to wobble back and forth. The first new planets found this way were the size of Jupiter and Neptune. Today we can detect smaller Earth-size worlds this way, too.

ET—TEXT HOME!

Our first attempt to locate alien life began in the 1960s, when astronomers turned radio telescopes toward space to listen for signals. Since then, we have listened to millions of stars hoping to catch an alien TV show like *Alien Idol* or the latest alien pop music. So far, we've picked up nothing. Not even a tweet!

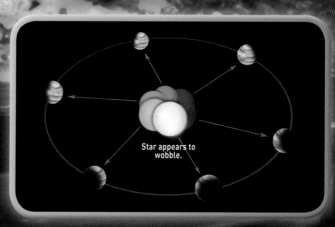

Star appears to wobble.

EVERYBODY SAY CHEESE

The latest way to find planets is to take their picture with a telescope. This can be difficult because stars are really bright, and planets are quite dim. The glare of the star can hide the tiny planet. But, if we put a small round disk in the telescope that blocks out the brighter starlight . . . Bingo! we can see a planet like this red-colored gas giant *(below)* located 230 light-years from Earth. With bigger telescopes, planets will be easier to photograph.

Star slightly dims when
the planet crosses it.

CAUTION: PLANETS CROSSING

Ever watch bugs fly around a light at night? This is another way astronomers find new planets. They measure the brightness of a distant star and then wait for a planet to cross in front of it like a bug. When this happens, the starlight dims slightly. Bigger planets cause stars to dim more than smaller planets. How often the dimming takes place reveals the orbit of the planet too.

Gas giant planet

WHAT TYPES OF "EARTH-LIKE" PLANETS ARE WE LOOKING FOR?

Earth is the only planet we know of that has life on it. Our next-door neighbors, Venus and Mars, are barren and lifeless. There may be creatures swimming in the oceans of Jupiter's moon Europa, or sliding around the frozen methane lakes of Saturn's moon Titan, but neither of these moons will have the diversity and variety of life found on Earth. To find planets with possible intelligent life on them, we must travel to the distant stars.

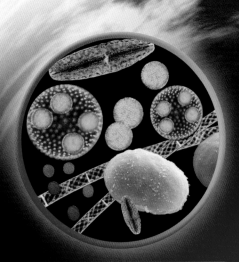

AN OXYGEN-RICH ATMOSPHERE

Take a deep breath. Now let it out. You just inhaled Earth's unique atmospheric mix: 21 percent oxygen, 78 percent nitrogen, and 1 percent other gases. The most important, oxygen, keeps us alive. Without it, living cells cannot change food into energy. And here's the funny part. Oxygen does not occur naturally here on Earth. Green plants create most of the oxygen we breathe as a waste product. So an alien planet with oxygen in its atmosphere will have something resembling plants living there too. The presence of oxygen will be the best clue that a world has life on it.

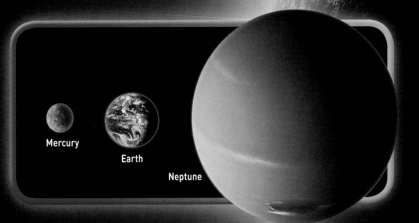

Mercury

Earth

Neptune

SIZE MATTERS

At 7,900 miles (12,700 km) in diameter, Earth is the perfect size for life. Planets smaller than Earth may not have enough gravity to hold an atmosphere. The air on these worlds would float away like a helium balloon. Planets four times as large as Earth turn into frozen balls of ice and gas like Uranus and Neptune. So, the size of a planet matters when searching for alien life.

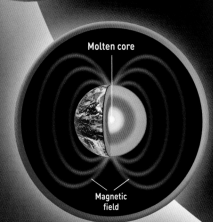

Molten core

Magnetic field

IRON CORES & MAGNETIC FIELDS

You can't feel the protective magnetic shield that surrounds Earth, but if it weren't there, we wouldn't be here either. Generated by Earth's molten iron core, this magnetic field protects us from deadly solar radiation. When a monster solar flare blasts off the surface of the sun, our magnetic field deflects it like Iron Man's metal suit. When this happens, we see aurora dancing across the night sky. For life to survive on an alien world, it will need a protective shield like ours.

VOLCANOES & EARTHQUAKES

Most people do not want rattling earthquakes or rumbling volcanoes popping up in their front yards. But for life to survive on a planet, volcanoes and planet quakes are a good thing. On Earth, the land we live on is made up of large continental plates that float over the ocean bottom. Where different plates crash together, carbon dioxide trapped in rocks and seashells gets buried deep underground. This helps maintain our moderately warm atmosphere. Too little carbon dioxide in the air and a planet freezes; too much and the planet cooks. Earthquakes and volcanoes, caused by these plates smashing into each other, are part of this life-protecting process!

MOST LIKELY TYPES OF ALIEN WORLDS

Moon

Super Earth

Terrestrial world

Ice world

Water world

Desert world

HABITABLE PLANETS

A habitable planet or moon is a world where conditions support life over long periods of time. These worlds fall into four basic categories: terrestrial Earth-like planets—both Earth-size and larger (super Earths)—with oceans and continents; more arid Mars-like desert planets; water worlds completely covered by oceans; and Europa-like planets with deep oceans covered by a shell of thick ice.

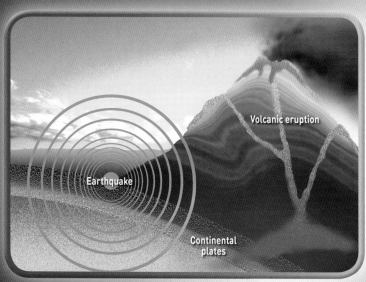

Volcanic eruption

Earthquake

Continental plates

HOW OLD ARE YOU?

When it comes to ice cream, age doesn't matter. Everybody likes it! When we search for life on other planets, age does matter. It took 4½ billion years for intelligent life to develop on Earth. On planets much younger than Earth, we might find single-celled plants and bacteria but nothing skateboarding or playing video games. On planets billions of years older than Earth, life may be coming to an end. As sun-like stars grow older, they get hotter. As they get hotter, they get bigger and turn red. We call them red giants. They swell in size and cook their inner planets. When searching for life in space, astronomers look for planets about the same age as Earth.

15

SWEET MYSTERY OF LIFE, HOW DO WE FIND YOU?

Are you ready for this? There is more to life than what we see around us. In fact, there may be more critters living in the Earth's crust than on the surface. On Earth, microbes live in our bodies, inside rocks, deep in the crust almost a mile (1.6 km) underground, in the clouds above our heads, and even on spacecraft launched into space. Once life begins, unless you melt the planet down, it is almost impossible to destroy. Even after our sun turns into a red giant and bakes the surface of Earth clean of all life, microbes will continue to survive hidden deep underground for billions of years to come.

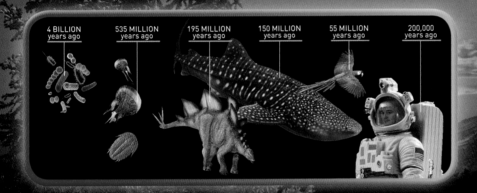

4 BILLION years ago | 535 MILLION years ago | 195 MILLION years ago | 150 MILLION years ago | 55 MILLION years ago | 200,000 years ago

LIFE BEGINS SIMPLE

The oldest fossils on Earth reveal that life began as single-celled organisms that evolved to more complex forms over time. Since the laws of physics are the same everywhere in the universe, we expect this pattern of simple to complex life will happen on alien planets too.

During the first 4 billion years on Earth, nothing exciting walked, flew, or swam in the seas. Then, at the end of a terrible ice age just 260 million years ago, the advanced complex life that includes all of us suddenly became part of the landscape of life on planet Earth.

LIFE NEEDS ENERGY

All forms of life need energy to survive. The food we eat supplies the energy we need to grow. Plants take in sunlight and need minerals absorbed from the soil and water to grow. Their leaves contain the pigment chlorophyll that captures sunlight and turns it into energy. Plant leaves are green solar cells. Put a plant in a dark room and it dies. Animals eat plants to gain the chemical energy stored in them. On Earth, plants and animals are closely connected in the energy cycle. On alien planets, we expect to see similar relationships.

RULES OF LIFE

All living things have special senses to protect themselves. Some trees know when insects are munching their leaves and produce poisons to stop them. Bats emit squeaky sounds that bounce off of insects to locate them in the dark. Bumblebees see ultraviolet light that helps them select the flower with the best pollen. Butterflies have magnetic wing scales that look like shingles on a roof to help them navigate long distances. Snakes have heat sensors on their tongues to locate prey at night. The aliens we meet will have special senses too—just wait and see!

BIGGER BRAINS NOT NEEDED

Everybody knows it is our big brain that makes us special. On Earth, it's cool to be a brainiac! But big brains are not a guarantee for survival. Bacteria and plants have no brains and they are the oldest living life on Earth. Starfish and jellyfish don't have brains and they do just fine. Worms and insects don't have much in the thinking department, but they have been around a long time. So, really, brains are not that big a deal when it comes to survival in the universe. They just make you more interesting to talk to.

Surrounded by water, smoking volcanic landmasses splashed with green life project above the tranquil seas. From orbit it's hard to detect that alien sea life is abundant here. The weather is calm today on Siluriana, but in a few short months the global hurricane season will begin making it extremely dangerous to explore.

OCEAN WORLD

Siluriana (sigh-LUR-ee-ana) with its copper-colored moon is a young super Earth covered by a sparkling blue sea. Located 30 light-years from Earth, this water world has almost twice the gravity as home, so take your time exploring. If you weigh 75 pounds on Earth, your weight will double to 150 pounds here, which will definitely slow you down. The air on Siluriana is breathable but contains less oxygen than we are used to. Located closer to its star than Earth is to our sun, the air is a sweltering 110°F (43°C). Wear your cooling suit when venturing onto land! While hiking, you will encounter sharp black volcanic rocks, a few black sand beaches, and large pools of fresh water. The only sounds here are the winds, lightly falling raindrops, and ocean waves crashing against the rocks. If we went back in time and visited Earth 450 million years ago, life would look a lot like what we find on Siluriana. A few million years from now, the planet's expanding continents will become home to life that has migrated from the ocean onto land.

The emerging volcanic rocks are safe to walk on. Vile greenbags abound—tall plant-like creatures filled with a foul-smelling slime that can sting for hours. Do not collect them without wearing carbon gloves. Waterchirpers feeding on greenbags can bite but typically scurry back into the water if approached. Listen for their high-pitched songs, which sound almost like sparrows' calls.

TYPE OF PLANET	SUPER EARTH
DIAMETER OF PLANET	11,800 MILES (18,990 KM)
GRAVITY	2x EARTH
AGE	4 BILLION YEARS OLD
ORBIT	92 MILLION MILES (148,059,648 KM)
LENGTH OF YEAR	299 DAYS
TEMPERATURE RANGE	85° TO 110° F (29° TO 43°C)
TYPE OF SUN	YOUNGER G STAR

Like people, habitable planets go through a series of changes in their lifetimes. Earth-like planets begin as molten rock that eventually cools down. Escaping steam during this cooling period condenses into rain that fills the ocean basins with water. Volcanoes rising out of the seas help build future landmasses or continents. On Earth, oceans now cover 71 percent of the surface. However, Siluriana is younger than our planet and future continents are just forming, so nearly 100 percent of its surface is covered with water. On Earth, life originated in the oceans and eventually migrated onto land. This same pattern is now happening on Siluriana. So let's go swimming and get ready to say hello! Just what types of alien life might we find here?

ARROWHEAD

Almost 70 feet (21 m) in length, and frightening as a bad dream, arrowheads are the most fearsome creatures on Siluriana. They weigh more than 100 tons (91 tonnes), and their massive dagger teeth measure almost 14 inches (36 cm) long! They are named for their distinct arrow-shaped heads, which make them look like swimming dragons.

GREENBAG

Somewhere between earthworms and bags of green burning slime in appearance, greenbags are animals, not plants. Inching slowly out of the water, they shoot out threads of protein glue that bind them to rocks. They feed on the small scraps of food left behind by the more mobile waterchirpers.

BIG BLUE MEANIE

Big blue meanies are blue-black in color, stand almost 6 feet (2 m) tall, and look like a cross between a daddy longlegs and an Alaskan king crab. They live on the ocean bottom and rarely venture into shallow waters. Using pairs of internal organs to pass electrolytes back and forth inside their bodies, they generate electric currents that can be fatal to their prey and to humans.

MOHAWK

Mohawks can reach 7 feet (2+ m) in size. They resemble water-breathing turtles without shells. Their name comes from the deadly poison spines on their backs that resemble the popular Native American haircut. While mohawks swim, these spines lay flat. When threatened, they jut straight up, defending the mohawk from attackers.

WATERCHIRPER

Scurrying across the rocks like mice, waterchirpers are the first large creatures to venture out of water onto land. They trap seawater inside their bodies, which surround the gills they still possess. It's almost as if they are wearing survival space suits too. Their name comes from the funny sounds they make while eating.

A young arrowhead about 30 feet (9 m) in length is learning a painful lesson. Believing he has an easy dinner in sight, he zeroes in on an alert mohawk. One bite of those poison spines, however, and the arrowhead has lost the battle—although he will live to find a safer meal. At this point in time on Siluriana, the oceans are the playgrounds for life. There are no large creatures roaming the newly rising continents. There are no plants or trees growing or creatures flying in the skies. All that will come later. For now, it's the oceans where we find all the active alien life.

Land formation on water planets is a long, slow process that continues throughout the planet's lifetime. Some newly discovered Earth-size planets are covered completely by oceans and don't have any land on them. On these worlds there may never be intelligent creatures that use technologies like we do, because it is really difficult to light a fire or plug in a toaster underwater!

INFRARED WORLD

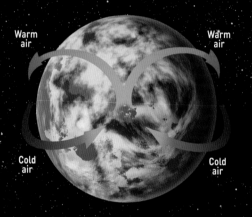

Warm air

Warm air

Cold air

Cold air

Warm air heated by its sun rises on the dayside of Yelrihs and flows toward the dark, cooler side of the planet. In turn, frigid air from the nightside rushes in to replace the rising warm air. This results in constant winds and tornadoes where cold and warm air meet along the twilight ring of this planet.

A t first, Yelrihs-57e (yell-rise) looks like Earth. But look closer. It has purple oceans and pink clouds. This shift in color comes from the tiny red dwarf star it orbits. About one-sixth the size of our sun, red dwarf stars shine for trillions, not billions, of years. Cooler in temperature, their habitable zones are much closer in than ours. Earth's habitable zone is 93 million miles (149,668,992 km) away from our sun. Orbiting a mere 18 million miles (28,968,192 km) away, Yelrihs has become tidally locked to its star, just like the moon is to Earth. Because it spins once every time it orbits its star, one side of Yelrihs is always in daylight and the other side is always in darkness. Circling around the middle of this world from north to south is a 200-mile-wide (322 km) ring of land and water that is in constant twilight. Even though a year is only 49 days long, day and night last forever. On Yelrihs, there are no seasons, no sunrises or sunsets. The closer look shows Yelrihs-57e isn't like our bountiful Earth at all!

TYPE OF PLANET	ROCKY/WATER WORLD
DIAMETER OF PLANET	7,000 MILES (11,265 KM)
GRAVITY	.8x EARTH
AGE	8 BILLION YEARS OLD
ORBIT	18 MILLION MILES (28,968,192 KM)
LENGTH OF YEAR	49 DAYS
TEMPERATURE RANGE	-20° TO 130° F (-28° TO 54°C)
TYPE OF SUN	RED DWARF (M STAR)

Faintly visible on the night-side of Yelrihs is a polar ice cap the size of Antarctica. Tinted red by its dwarf star, the oceans appear purple to our eyes, and the clouds and sky look pink. It is just a bit smaller than Earth and has less gravity as well.

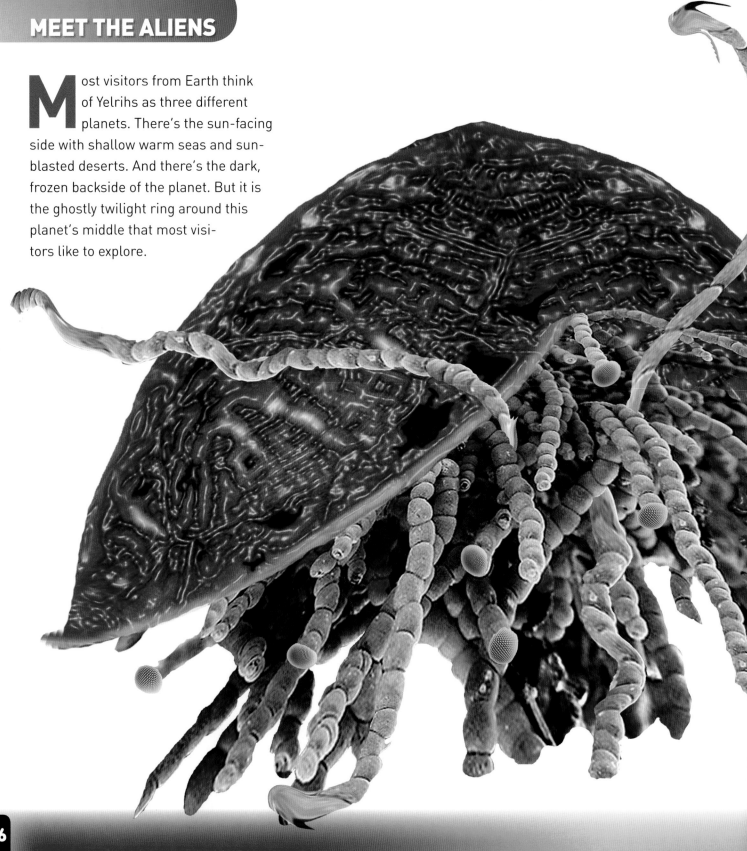

Most visitors from Earth think of Yelrihs as three different planets. There's the sun-facing side with shallow warm seas and sun-blasted deserts. And there's the dark, frozen backside of the planet. But it is the ghostly twilight ring around this planet's middle that most visitors like to explore.

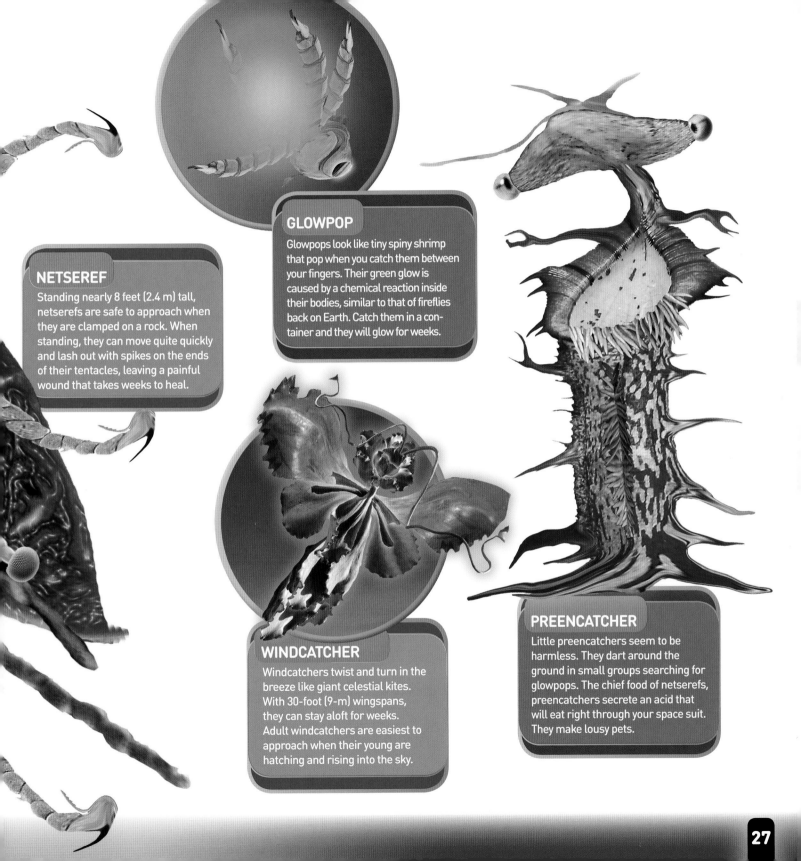

GLOWPOP

Glowpops look like tiny spiny shrimp that pop when you catch them between your fingers. Their green glow is caused by a chemical reaction inside their bodies, similar to that of fireflies back on Earth. Catch them in a container and they will glow for weeks.

NETSEREF

Standing nearly 8 feet (2.4 m) tall, netserefs are safe to approach when they are clamped on a rock. When standing, they can move quite quickly and lash out with spikes on the ends of their tentacles, leaving a painful wound that takes weeks to heal.

WINDCATCHER

Windcatchers twist and turn in the breeze like giant celestial kites. With 30-foot (9-m) wingspans, they can stay aloft for weeks. Adult windcatchers are easiest to approach when their young are hatching and rising into the sky.

PREENCATCHER

Little preencatchers seem to be harmless. They dart around the ground in small groups searching for glowpops. The chief food of netserefs, preencatchers secrete an acid that will eat right through your space suit. They make lousy pets.

Here in the twilight zone of Yelrihs, plants do not look like the foliage back home. Earth grasses and trees absorb red and blue wavelengths of sunlight for energy and reject incoming green light. Plants look green to us because green light is bouncing off the leaves back into our eyes. On Yelrihs, its star sends out energy mostly in infrared light instead of a rainbow of colors like our sun. Infrared energy is a form of light that our eyes cannot see but that we can feel. (When you open the door to a hot oven, the heat rushing out is infrared energy.) Our sun sends out infrared energy, too—it causes sun-burns. Here on Yelrihs, infra-red light makes plants appear black instead of green! And creatures with infrared eyes see this world quite differently from the way we see it.

Venturing into the dark nightside of Yelrihs, a netseref uses infrared sight to pierce the darkness and identify an unsuspecting prey. Meanwhile, in the distance, a twisting tornado has just dropped down onto this eerie landscape.

Chaos is one of eight moons orbiting the blue ice giant planet Wakanda, which means "multiplication" in Sioux. Vivid auroras dance across the night sky generated by a strong magnetic field that protects life from deadly radiation from both Wakanda and its distant sun, a very hot F star.

SATELLITE WORLD

This is a world where you never know what will happen next. Technically, Chaos isn't a planet. It is a moon orbiting a giant ice planet much like Uranus and Neptune. Ice giants are incapable of supporting life even if they form in the habitable zones of a star. But their moons can. If they are big enough to hold an atmosphere like Saturn's moon Titan, they could be crawling with life. Orbiting a hotter F star, Chaos is located farther away from its sun than we are from ours. Why is it named Chaos? On this lush tropical world, there are issues! Giant planets are natural magnets for comets and asteroids zipping their way through solar systems. Being a moon around one of these space magnets means you frequently get hit too. Giant planets also tug on their moons with gravitational fields. These interactions result in sporadic rumbling moonquakes and violently erupting volcanoes on Chaos. Add meteorites crashing down from above onto this continuously changing landscape and there it is—chaos.

Tidal forces between Wakanda and Chaos create ocean waves over 60 feet (18 m) tall. To escape the crushing force of these walls of water crashing onto the shoreline, beachrollers ride the ocean waves inside self-inflating crash balloons. Like the airbags in a car, the balloons soften the blow when waves break on the beach.

TYPE OF PLANET	ROCKY MOON
DIAMETER OF PLANET	7,120 MILES (11,459 KM)
GRAVITY	.7x EARTH
AGE	4.1 BILLION YEARS OLD
ORBIT	42 DAYS AROUND ICE GIANT
LENGTH OF YEAR	411 DAYS AROUND SUN
TEMPERATURE RANGE	40 TO 110°F (4.5° TO 43°C)
TYPE OF SUN	F STAR

MEET THE ALIENS

Lighter gravity on Chaos results in creatures that are taller and thinner. They can also move more rapidly, so be watchful when exploring during the day. Because Chaos is so warm, animal life has no need to generate body heat like mammals do back on Earth. No warm-blooded creatures have evolved here. When air temperatures cool down at night, life moves a bit slower as body temperatures decrease too.

ARTIPOD
What's that smell?! Exerting a scent similar to the nectar of fungoids, clever artipods are hunters that position themselves near fungoids and wait for an unsuspecting antilla to stray into their trap. Within minutes, a struggling antilla can become a satisfying snack for an artipod!

ANTILLA
Antillas are 10-foot-tall (3 m) creatures that move very quickly through the jungles following invisible odor trails left behind by advance scouts. Ferocious warriors, they protect the fungoids from predators. In turn, the fungoids produce nectars that feed and nourish antillas.

GREENSKIN
Greenskins are similar to Earth's salamanders and are masters at camouflage. Standing nearly 7 feet (2+ m) tall, these cold-blooded creatures lay eggs in ponds and streams that hatch out into young greenskins. Although they may look a little like humans, they do not use tools or make any sounds to communicate with one another.

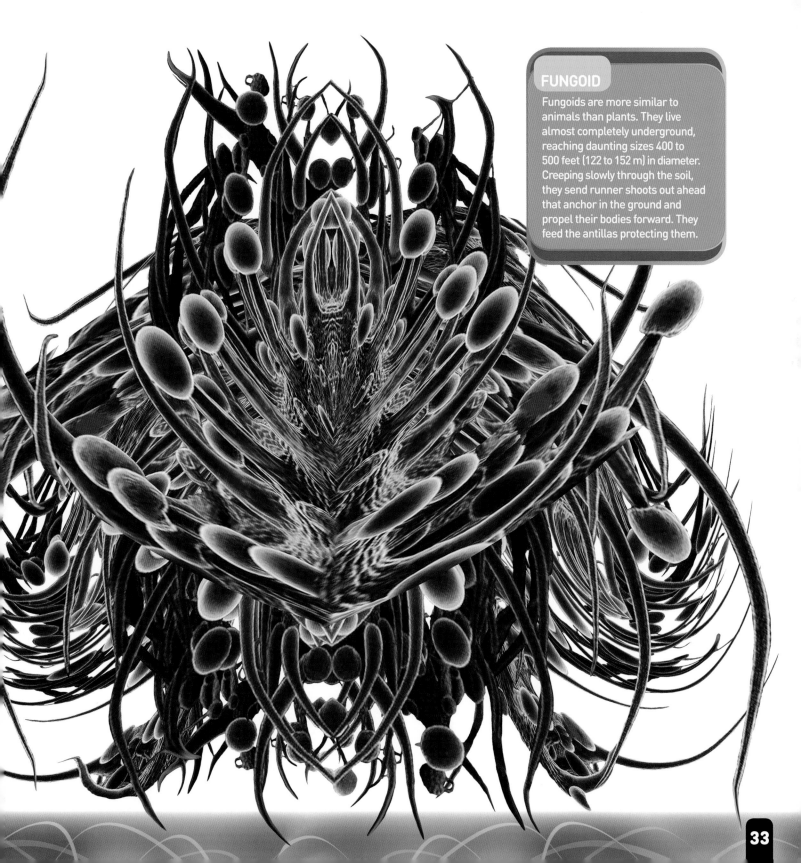

Chaos is a moon orbiting a host planet. This means there are two bright light sources in its sky. With its sun undergoing eclipses every six days and changing phases of Wakanda shining down on it, the intensity of daylight reaching Chaos changes continuously. These differences in daylight alter the wake and sleep cycles of life on this planet as well as when they hunt or hide from predators. These changes work out to the greenskins' advantage. By changing the color of their skin, they can almost disappear into their surroundings. Look closely. There are three greenskins in this image. Can you find all three?

Shown here, the ice giant planet Wakanda crosses the path of its sun creating a solar eclipse that plunges Chaos into total darkness. Like streetlights turning on at sunset, bioluminescent trees glow during this spectacular event.

DYING WORLD

After nearly 8 billion years of radiating sunlight, the life-supporting star that planet Moros orbits is dying. In these last few million years, it has grown steadily hotter as it runs out of hydrogen fuel. Now on Moros, oceans are dramatically receding and visibly turning brown from all the dust in the air. Its grand rivers are withering and the atmosphere has become unbearably hot and brutal. Once lush, this world is now transforming into a global barren desert. Sand dunes and bare rock now shape the landscape of this changing world. Water on Moros is dangerously scarce. Creatures here have adapted by evolving new methods to protect themselves from the intense heat and diminishing water supply. Many venture out only at night or burrow deep underground to stay cool. Some store water like a cactus does on Earth. Armed with insulating shells and thick skins, alien life valiantly survives. Here on Moros, we are getting a glimpse of our own fate. In the next few billion years, as our sun begins running out of hydrogen fuel, it will grow hotter and begin transforming Earth into a world much like Moros.

A massive sandstorm bears down on a starcreeper that has discovered a pocket of water hidden beneath the sand. With its body now inflated like a water balloon, it cannot move fast enough to escape and will have to wait out the storm.

TYPE OF PLANET	ROCKY SUPER EARTH
DIAMETER OF PLANET	12,450 MILES (20,036 KM)
GRAVITY	2.1x EARTH
AGE	5.9 BILLION YEARS OLD
ORBIT	94 MILLION MILES (151,278,336 KM)
LENGTH OF YEAR	390 DAYS
TEMPERATURE RANGE	85° TO 140°F (29° TO 60°C)
TYPE OF SUN	OLDER G STAR

Moros is a planet that is growing old. Like all living things, planets have life spans too. Most Earth-like worlds experience a period of about 4 to 5 billion years for life to flourish before rising temperatures cause plants to start dying off. Soon, the animals that eat the plants disappear too. In the very end, the last to go are the tiny bacteria.

Here on Moros, the pull of gravity is twice that of Earth. Watch out—this means your Earth weight is doubled here, and you didn't even have that extra piece of pizza! Always wear your gravity-assist suits while hiking this vast terrain. Aliens here have bodies that are more compressed and lower to the ground than creatures back home (another by-product of super gravity). Most awaken and mobilize between sunset and dawn. Here we see two interesting examples of radial symmetry. Both starcreepers and tripids have bodies that radiate from a central point, much like a starfish. On Earth, this body type is only found in the oceans.

TRIPIDS

Tripids are big and heavy and move without walking. Their mouths are supported by three stout legs on pedestals. They glide easily across the sand, like sidewinders. They have no eyes or ears; they sense the world instead through sonar waves and radar beams. Tripids have the distinction of being the only three-legged creatures in the known universe.

WABALONE

Wabalones are highly intelligent and big! Comparable in size to small elephants, they have thick shells, which protect them from destructive infrared and gamma rays emitted by Moros's dying sun. Nomads of the desert, they feed like mosquitoes on starcreepers filled with water. They live longer than most aliens and communicate through their feet with low-frequency sounds that travel **underground** for miles. Humans can't hear these sounds, so we miss all the good wabalone jokes!

CAVE CRAWLER

Cave crawlers are scavengers that live in deep underground caverns and tunnels to escape the rising surface temperatures. They are roughly the size of soccer balls, and their multiple eyes can see in near darkness. They also have a nasty bite.

STARCREEPER

Because of its radial shape (like spokes on a bicycle tire), you might mistake a starcreeper for a starfish stranded in the desert. Underneath its arms are tiny probes that penetrate deep into the sand searching for water. If it finds a pocket of water, it draws it up and stores it inside, much like a desert cactus.

LIFE ON THE SURFACE

Most of the larger inhabitants, including the trees and plants of this expiring world, perished long ago. Only the toughest and best adapted creatures remain now. This is a world running in reverse and for the years to come, only the hardiest will survive. The forecast is gloomy for the future of life on Moros, but this is the natural course of all living planets, including our own Earth 3 billion years from now. On Moros the golden age of life is now reaching its end.

As lightning illuminates the sky, a group of wabalones begin their nocturnal forage for food and water. In the distance, two younger ones examine a giant shell of one of their ancient ancestors. It is a reminder of an earlier time when Moros was more hospitable to life.

41

Arclandia is a rocky water world locked in a perpetual ice age. Due to an 11-degree tilt to its axis, seasonal changes warm it up enough in summertime for ice on the southern continent to melt, exposing barren ground.

DOUBLE WORLD

Imagine two alien worlds, slightly younger than Earth, occupying the same habitable zone around the same sun-like star. In 2013, astronomers made the first discovery of such a system—named Kepler-62e and 62f. Our two planets are called Venera and Arclandia. There are only 2 million miles (3,218,688 km) separating them, or a little more than eight times the distance between the moon and Earth. If you were to fly in an old moon rocket, you could make the run from one to the other in 12 days. Both of these worlds shine brightly in the night sky, but for different reasons. Closer to its sun, Venera is shrouded in thick, bright sun-reflecting clouds. It also rains a lot on Venera. Farther out, where it is colder, sunlight reflects from the dazzling white sheets of ice that cover the landscape of Arclandia. Imagine Venera and Arclandia as twins, where one lives in the tropics and the other at the North Pole.

Radar probes placed in orbit around Venera use pulses of energy to penetrate the thick clouds and monitor the surface below. Landing on Venera can be tricky. The top cloud layers rip along at almost 800 miles (1,288 km) an hour. On the surface, visibility is considered good if you can see 20 feet (6 m) in front of you!

	VENERA	ARCLANDIA
TYPE OF PLANET	ROCKY WATER WORLD	ROCKY WATER WORLD
DIAMETER OF PLANET	8,900 MILES (14,323 KM)	11,300 MILES (18,186 KM)
GRAVITY	1x EARTH	1.4x EARTH
AGE	4.3 BILLION YEARS OLD	4.3 BILLION YEARS OLD
ORBIT	92 MILLION MILES (148,059,648 KM)	94 MILLION MILES (151,278,336 KM)
LENGTH OF YEAR	220 DAYS	388 DAYS
TEMPERATURE RANGE	65° TO 118°F (18° TO 48°C)	-25° TO 45°F (-32° TO 7°C)
TYPE OF SUN	G STAR	G STAR

Nestled just inside the outer limits of its star's habitable zone, Arclandia is an Earth-like planet of sweeping expanses and radiant natural beauty. Life here resembles creatures from Earth's long-ago ice ages. Gravity's forces are a bit stronger than back home, resulting in aliens with larger legs to help support their weight. The six-legged animals here are an evolutionary response to a more powerful gravitational field. Here we also confront the most ferocious and cunning beast of any planet, the arctic dregaes.

OBAKI

Obakis are ten-armed shape shifters. Devoid of a skeleton, they can assume nearly any shape, both in the water and on dry land. In water, they secrete a milky substance that serves as a fishing net for catching prey. Each of their arms has a mouth at the end of it, and rows of light-sensing eyes line these arms.

SEAPUP

Seapups are friendly beasts with a fun sense of humor. What looks like a big pink tongue hanging down in front is actually a pair of curled-up feelers with sharp little side hooks used to spear small obakis in the water. Do not be surprised if you turn your back while exploring and feel something tickling you. They seem to enjoy doing this to humans and each other over and over again.

ARCTIC DREGAES

The arctic dregaes (DRA-gus) is an agile, warm-blooded hunter, capable of outrunning any human being. Larger than a minivan and weighing up to 600 pounds (272 kg), its golden head plate can detect vibrations caused by distant movements. Incredibly, this brute can pick up the footsteps of a mouse-size creature 300 feet (91 m) away. If you see one, do not move!

THUNDERBEAST

Thunderbeasts are muscular six-legged creatures that stand 14 feet (4 m) tall and weigh nearly 2 tons (1.8 tonnes) when fully grown. Females are much larger than males and have massive spiked horns. The females watch over herds of smaller males to protect them. Males are easily identi-fied because they lack the female's powerful horns.

LIFE ON THE SURFACE

Two distant moons shine down on a family of grazing thunderbeasts. Here daytime temperatures may reach a toasty, for Arclandia, 40°F (4.5°C). Increased gravity not only affects the shape of animals, it influences the height of plant life too. No giant redwood type forests are found here. The advantage to being a hexapod ("hex" means six and "pod" means foot) is that any stress on its leg bones due to stronger gravity is spread out, thereby reducing the possibility of breakage.

A seapup sits on an ice floe, feasting on a freshly caught small obaki. Clearly visible, its two blue lung sacs act as sea floats while angling. On dry land, they deflate and align close to its body, much like a life jacket.

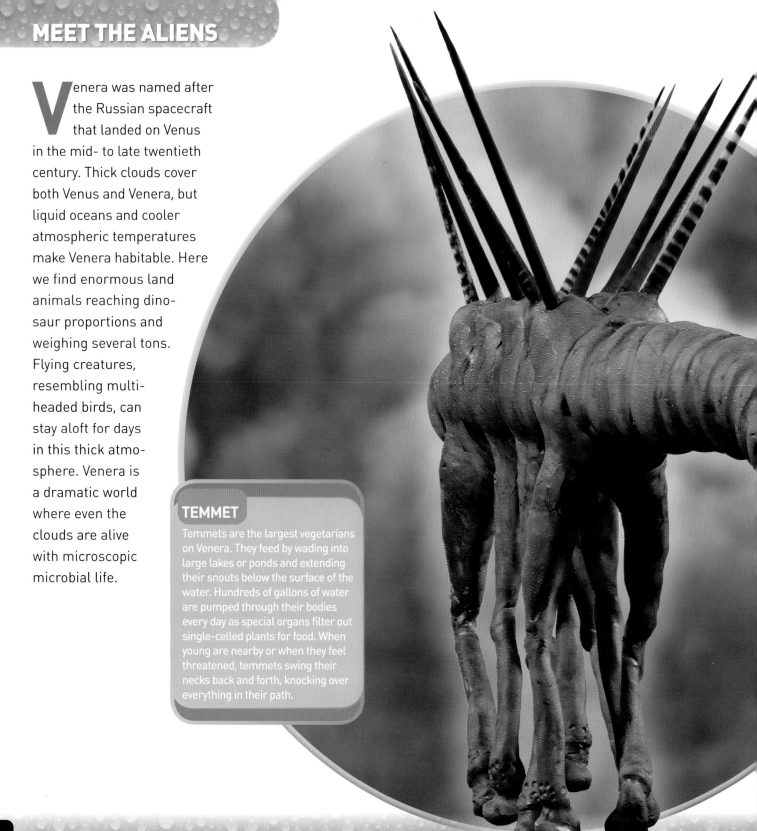

Venera was named after the Russian spacecraft that landed on Venus in the mid- to late twentieth century. Thick clouds cover both Venus and Venera, but liquid oceans and cooler atmospheric temperatures make Venera habitable. Here we find enormous land animals reaching dinosaur proportions and weighing several tons. Flying creatures, resembling multi-headed birds, can stay aloft for days in this thick atmosphere. Venera is a dramatic world where even the clouds are alive with microscopic microbial life.

TEMMET

Temmets are the largest vegetarians on Venera. They feed by wading into large lakes or ponds and extending their snouts below the surface of the water. Hundreds of gallons of water are pumped through their bodies every day as special organs filter out single-celled plants for food. When young are nearby or when they feel threatened, temmets swing their necks back and forth, knocking over everything in their path.

IBONG

Ibongs are bird-like creatures that change colors as they fly. Biologists believe the color shifts are used as a means to communicate with one another. With 12-foot (4-m) wing-spans, their multiple heads spit tiny balls of fire at their prey, hitting them up to 30 feet (9 m) away.

KASA-OBAKE

Kasa-obakes, the Japanese name for an ancient creature that looked like an umbrella, taste and eat decaying material through their feet. They have no mouths. They wear their skeletons on the outside of their bodies in the form of lightweight round shields that are made out of tightly woven strands of hair.

CONEHEAD

Coneheads are social creatures standing almost 10 feet (3 m) tall. Like dogs, they have a remarkable sense of smell. Scientists believe their main mode of communication is through odors exchanged between them. When approached by humans, they can become quite agitated if we forget and wear perfume or cologne.

LIFE ON THE SURFACE

Life on Venera is hard for humans to adapt to. Steam rising from fissures in the ground shows Venera is still volcanically active. Rain falling continuously makes this world of ghostly wonders bleak and wet. Shrouded in thick fog and swirling clouds, nothing stays dry for very long. Life-forms here don't depend upon eyesight like humans do. It's just too cloudy to see anything. Instead, other senses guide their lives. Some creatures use sonar to find their way around, like bats and whales do. Others, called "smellers," have unbelievably sensitive noses that reveal their world to them in much the same way that eyes do for humans.

Ambling across a barren rocky canyon, an older temmet, with a few broken spikes, searches for water. Some of these gentle giants reach 50 feet (15 m) in length and weigh more than 20 tons (18 tonnes). The spikes on their backs are not for protection. Instead of depending on eyesight, small pulses of radar are sent out from the tips of the spikes to help them visualize their way.

METAMORPHIC WORLD

The orbit of Hypnos resembles a Hula-Hoop somebody stepped on! As it swings close to its star, Hypnos picks up orbital speed before zooming back out to the colder reaches of its solar system. On its closest approach, it is about the same distance Earth is from our sun. At its farthest point, it would reach near the orbit of Ceres in our asteroid belt.

Sleepy Hypnos is a planet that goes silent for three years before it suddenly awakens with the arrival of spring. Then, as if wonderfully refreshed, it quickly thaws and flourishes in vibrant summer weather. Much too quickly, fall arrives and Hypnos slips back into a deep, cold, undisturbed sleep. These radical changes are due to the unusual orbit it has around its star. Instead of a circular one like Earth's, Hypnos has a long elliptical orbit, a result of a collision with another planetary body when it formed. Since there are no gas giants like Jupiter in this solar system to stabilize orbits, the odd annual trek it makes around its sun remains unchanged. In winter, thick ice forms on top of the oceans and lakes, sealing everything in underneath this arctic surface. Very few creatures on the surface remain active during this chillingly cold period. However, some have found a unique way to deal with these extreme environmental changes. Like a caterpillar transforming into a butterfly, they alter their shapes and become something new and different.

TYPE OF PLANET	SUPER EARTH
DIAMETER OF PLANET	16,211 MILES (26,089 KM)
GRAVITY	2.1x EARTH
AGE	7.2 BILLION YEARS OLD
ORBIT	66,239,000 MILES TO 248,771,000 MILES (106,601,337 TO 400,358,116 km)
LENGTH OF YEAR	1,099 DAYS
TEMPERATURE RANGE	-159° TO 102° F (-106° TO 39° C)
TYPE OF SUN	K STAR & RED DWARF M STAR

Long-awaited spring arrives on Hypnos as it quickly shakes off its cold winter coat. Ice sheets give way to splashes of blue and green as far as the eye can see. Hypnos is renewed. Gone are the freezing temperatures. Every vista is now filled with fresh sounds of life awakening.

The Latin word "metamorphosis" means many forms or visible changes in an animal's appearance. Here on Earth, butterflies lay eggs that hatch as caterpillars who then spin cocoons and emerge as butter-flies. On Hypnos, there is a creature that demon-strates a different type of body change. It survives the long winters in one form, and as spring arrives, its body splits apart to reveal a profoundly new form. By fall, a hard shell forms, cycling it back into its winter survival shape.

MARMITE

During the long winters, ocean-swimming marmites are the primary food source of icecrawlers. Living their entire lifetime in less than 12 hours, marmites are the shortest-lived creatures on this planet. They are born and grow old before the sun sets. You can say life really flies by quickly for marmites.

ICECRAWLER

Resembling giant slugs, icecrawlers are one of two separate creatures that change with the harsh winters and brief summers on Hypnos. They possess unique biological charac-teristics. In wintertime, the fluids in their bodies contain a high degree of glucose, or sugar, that acts like the antifreeze in car radiators. This fluid keeps them from freezing too.

As temperatures start to rise and energy derived from sunlight increases, the thick outer skin of the icecrawler turns into a rigid outer shell. Inside, a miraculous transition is taking place. Within 48 hours, cracks will appear in the shell's hard exterior and new, spindly legs will jut out. Crawling slowly from its alien cocoon, a gorb emerges, ready to experience life during the warmth of summer.

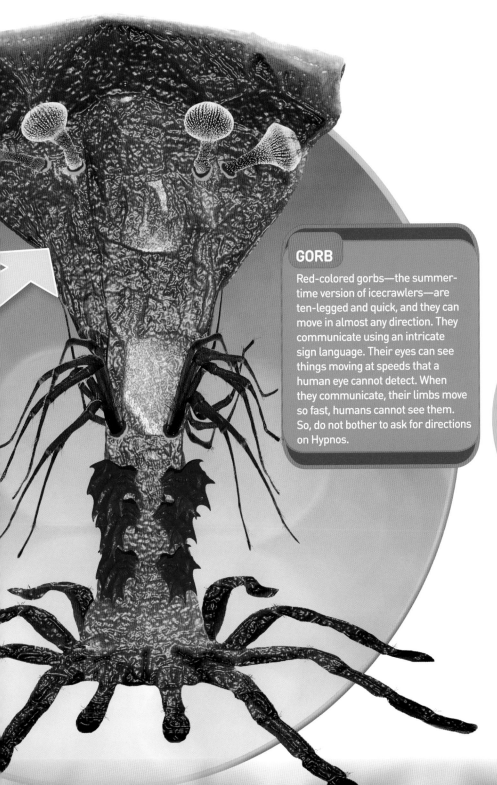

Sweet summer is short on Hypnos! Ice fields and frozen lakes melt rapidly, becoming bright fields of green- and maize-colored alien flowers and grasses. Once awakened from winter slumber, this planetary landscape bursts forth lightning fast into full summer.

GORB

Red-colored gorbs—the summer-time version of icecrawlers—are ten-legged and quick, and they can move in almost any direction. They communicate using an intricate sign language. Their eyes can see things moving at speeds that a human eye cannot detect. When they communicate, their limbs move so fast, humans cannot see them. So, do not bother to ask for directions on Hypnos.

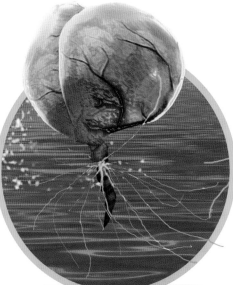

WINDWALKER

Windwalkers are the butterflies of Hypnos. Instead of wings, they have two flexible air sacs inflated with hydrogen gas. Skillfully surviving the winter by staying sealed in egg cases inside the ice, they fill the summertime skies of Hypnos like party balloons.

LIFE ON THE SURFACE

Hypnos becomes unimaginably cold when its orbit swings away from its star. At its farthest point, the entire planet freezes over, resembling Antarctica on Earth. Life on this world has developed many defenses to survive these extremes. Some creatures burrow deep underground and sleep until the warmth returns. Others move into the oceans, surviving under the ice. Only icecrawlers remain active on the surface.

Marmites are the main food source of icecrawlers. They undergo laser-fast cell growth that allows them to reach full maturity in just a few hours! Imagine if you were born in the morning, became a teenager by 10 a.m., an adult by noon, and a grandparent by last period in school. Now that would be an interesting day!

White clouds of hatching smits draw the attention of emerging windwalkers on this warm summer day. Everything on this world has evolved toward rapid growth and frenzied feeding in preparation for the long cold winter ahead. On Earth similar climates unfold in Alaska and Patagonia, but not on such a planetary scale. This is a world of two seasonal extremes—one a color-splashed summer, and the other a dark and desolate winter where ice storms can rage for months. Most visitors from Earth arrive during the busy spectacle of changes between spring and fall.

Not to be left out of the activities, plants undergo rapid growth spurts too. In a matter of hours, melting ice-cloaked valleys bloom into lush green panoramas where ruby-topped podtrees shoot up at a rate of 6 feet (2 m) a day. Landscapes photographed in the morning change remarkably by early afternoon.

The odd-shaped alien space station looks down on the vast array of green-lit tunnels leading to caverns deep beneath the surface of Chronos. Like a round ball with brightly lit windows, this planet travels through space illuminated by red clouds of hydrogen gas instead of a sun.

ROGUE WORLD

Chronos is the last stop on our cosmic journey, and it may be the strangest of all the alien planets we've encountered. In our quest to explore Earth-like alien worlds, Chronos is something we didn't expect. Instead of biological creatures made of flesh and blood, here we find creatures made of spun metal, ceramic glass, and glowing energy fields. They are living machines and something beyond. They survive on a dark world with no sun to warm it. There are no oceans or plants. It is a planet of bare rock and ice. A close encounter with a gas giant planet ages ago pushed Chronos out of its orbit, sending it hurtling through space all alone. For biological life, it was catastrophic. For intelligent synthetic life, it made no difference. This is a world inhabited by artificial life-forms that merged with intelligent biological organisms in the distant past . . . something scientists predict may happen someday to the human race. The vast reservoirs of energy that power this world are located near volcanic vents or deep underground. Even without a sun, artificial life survives in our universe.

Catastrophes happen even to planets. Looming large in the sky, a passing Jupiter-size planet sends moons crashing into Chronos. Ejected from its solar system and now traveling through space all alone, Chronos demonstrates how resilient life may be out there among the stars.

TYPE OF PLANET	ROCKY SUPER EARTH WITH THIN ATMOSPHERE
DIAMETER OF PLANET	8,800 MILES (14,162 KM)
GRAVITY	1.2x EARTH
AGE	5.2 BILLION YEARS OLD
ORBIT	NO ORBIT
LENGTH OF YEAR	NO YEARS RECORDED
TEMPERATURE	20°F (-6.7°C)
TYPE OF SUN	NO SUN

The universe was born out of the big bang 13.7 billion years ago. The first wave of life based on biology may have emerged quickly, within a few billion years after this cosmic event. Life on Earth appeared much later, around 4 billion years ago. The first wave of life in the universe was certainly composed of chemical protein chains that merged together to form simple units that reproduced, took in energy, released waste products, and responded to outside stimuli. On Chronos, we have uncovered the second wave of a life in the universe. This life is artificial and the next step beyond biological life.

ROCKET POD

Besides plentiful single-celled bacteria-size life-forms living in the soil and rocks, rocket pods are the only surviving biological life on Chronos. When touched, oval pods launch into the air with a bang, landing up to half a mile (0.8 km) away. Upon impact, baby rocket pods spring to life.
CAUTION: Do not stand in front of a rocket pod to test this out!

WALKING RAINBOWS

So much of this world is a mystery to us. Walking rainbows appear to be made out of a liquid that changes shape and color spontaneously. They interact with the master orbs in ways we don't quite understand. One theory is that they are young master orbs. Another theory says they are master orb pets. What do you think?

ROBODRILLER

Almost 7 feet (2+ m) tall, robodrillers are robots that relentlessly mine their world for precious building materials. When one breaks down, repair robots appear to fix it moments later. Like worker bees in a hive, they are all interconnected to some central controlling computer.

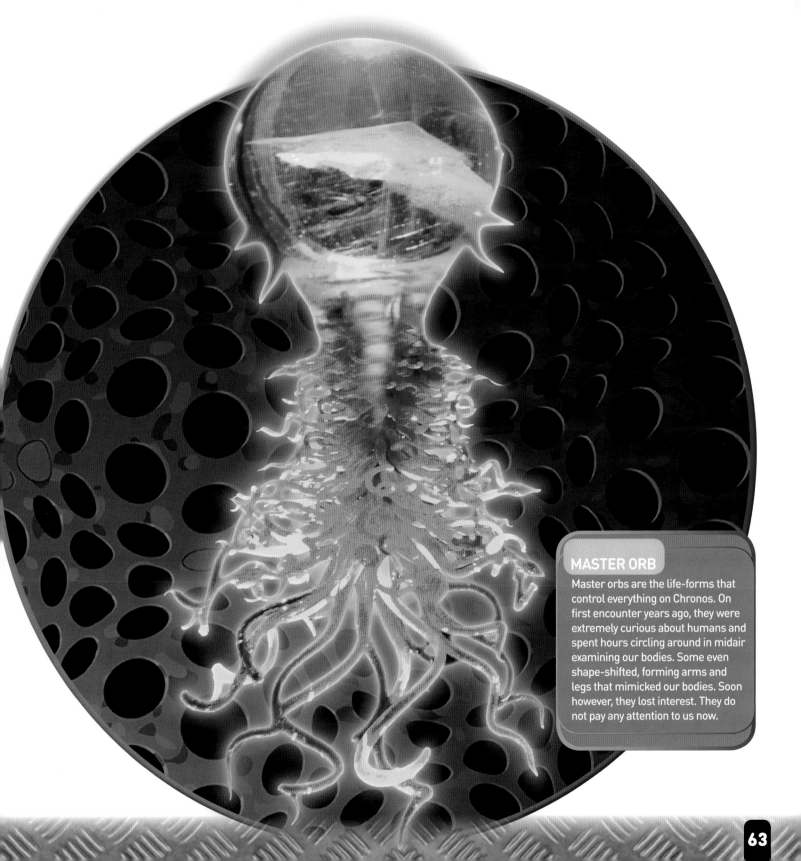

MASTER ORB

Master orbs are the life-forms that control everything on Chronos. On first encounter years ago, they were extremely curious about humans and spent hours circling around in midair examining our bodies. Some even shape-shifted, forming arms and legs that mimicked our bodies. Soon however, they lost interest. They do not pay any attention to us now.

When Chronos was discovered, the grand mystery was trying to determine what type of life we had stumbled upon. The second mystery was what were they doing to their world? Chronos is riddled with thousands of miles of tunnels and mine shafts. But why? The answer is stunning. The inhabitants of Chronos are turning their world into a steerable spaceship that will take them to destinations somewhere else in the universe. The first artificial life we've discovered in the cosmos is on a mission to travel the stars, and we don't know where they are going—not yet!

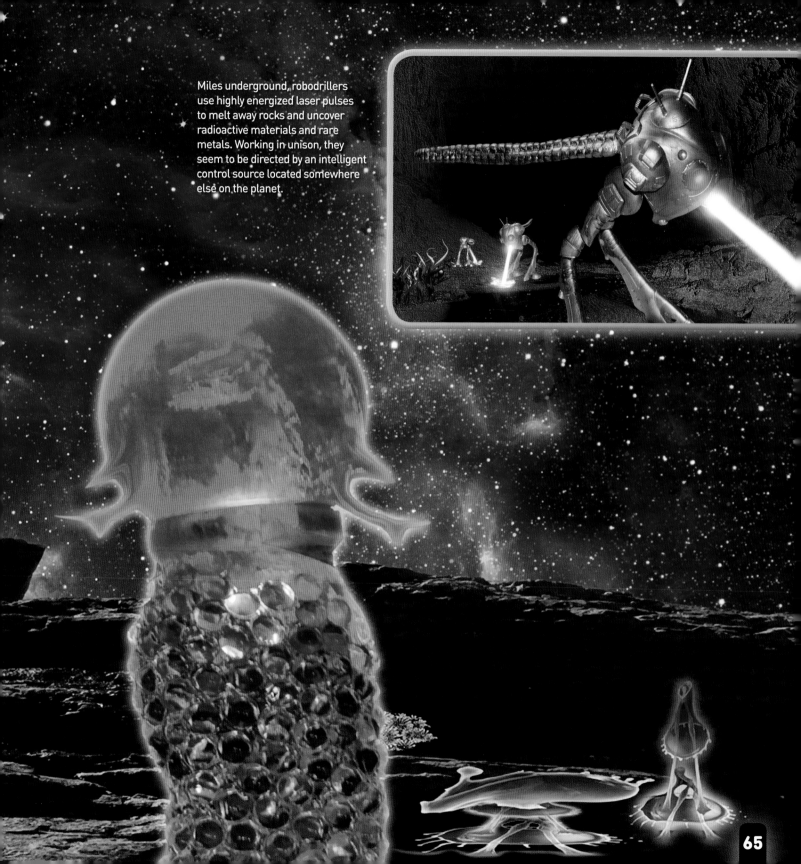

Miles underground, robodrillers use highly energized laser pulses to melt away rocks and uncover radioactive materials and rare metals. Working in unison, they seem to be directed by an intelligent control source located somewhere else on the planet.

CONCLUSION: FIRST ENCOUNTERS

Sometime this century, an interstellar spaceship bound for a distant star system may become a reality. To find other Earth-like planets that can support life, we must search far beyond our own solar system. Scientists are now discovering new Earth-like planets at a rapid rate, and eventually we will detect life on one of them. With this discovery, the greatest adventure in human history will have begun. The spirit of humankind propels us to answer one of the most profound questions ever asked: Are we alone? Designing spacecraft to reach the stars will be a remarkable technical achievement. The length of the journey will be so long that it may be measured in decades or centuries. Yet that will be the cost of discovering who our neighbors are and just how diverse life is in our Milky Way galaxy.

Traveling more than 26 trillion miles (42 trillion km) through space, the first interstellar probe from Earth arrives at the Alpha Centauri system, which is composed of three suns, not one. Zooming past an Earth-size planet orbiting the orange-colored star Alpha Centauri B, two robotic explorers jet away. Their mission: to beam back the first images of alien life from this cool outer planet.

HOW TO BUILD YOUR OWN ALIEN

MAKING AN ALIEN

Try your hand at creating your own alien! To create some of the aliens in this book, I used polymer clay. This material is non-toxic, washes clean with soap and water, and is easy to work with. It comes in different colors and stays pliable for weeks, turning hard only when baked in the oven. Then it can be sanded, carved, and painted with acrylic paints.

First, form your clay into figures. You can roll your clay out into thin flat sheets by using a kitchen rolling pin, or even a pasta maker, which works great on clay. An old butter knife is handy for cutting clay into smaller pieces.

Next, detail your alien. Your tools do not need to be anything special. The most useful instruments for smoothing, blending, and texturing (either when the clay is soft or baked) are small and medium-size aluminum knitting needles. You can also use toothpicks, old combs, darning needles, pieces of wire, or anything else you come across to texture surfaces.

When your figures are formed, place them in a glass or aluminum dish and bake at 275°F (135°C), but no higher, for one hour. Be certain to get permission to use the oven! After an hour, turn the oven off and let the clay slowly cool inside the oven. If you take it out while it is still warm, it may bend or break.

After it cools, it's time to decorate and paint. If you wish, you can glue on pieces of any material to bring your alien to life!

MATERIALS AND TOOLS

1 to 2 POUNDS (0.5 to 1 KG) POLYMER CLAY (your choice of colors)

ALUMINUM FOIL

THIN BEADING WIRE (for legs, arms, and tails)

SMALL WIRE CUTTERS/BUTTER KNIFE

ROLLING PIN or PASTA MAKER

TOOTHPICKS or LARGE DARNING NEEDLE (for texturing)

RULER

WHITE WATER-SOLUBLE MULTIPURPOSE GLUE

ACRYLIC PAINTS

PAINTBRUSHES (small and large)

REFERENCE BOOKS (or your own imagination)

1 GETTING STARTED

First you must condition the clay. Knead it together with your hands for a few minutes, or run it through your pasta machine 15 to 20 times to make it soft and pliable.

2 SHAPING THE FOIL CORE

Use a sheet of aluminum foil 12" wide by 16" long (30 cm x 40 cm) and crumple it up into a ball as tightly as you can. Roll the ball firmly against a tabletop or use a small hammer to make it round and smooth.

3 COVERING THE FOIL CORE

Press small pieces of clay around the foil ball and blend them in with your thumbs until no aluminum foil is showing. Blend the edges with your fingers to smooth them out. When completely covered, apply a full sheet of clay as a wrapping layer over the top of the first layer, blending in the edges. Smooth out any lumps or imperfections by rolling it gently on a tabletop.

4 MAKING THE LEGS

Cut six equal rectangles of clay from a ⅛"-thick (3 mm) sheet approximately 1.5" by 5" (38 mm x 127 mm) and roll each one between the palms of your hands into an extended egg tapered smaller on one end. These will become your six legs.

5 MAKING THE BOTTOM RING

Cut a piece of clay ½" by 1" (12 mm x 25 mm). Roll it between your palms into a thin rope. Circle the rope on the bottom part of the body as shown. Using your knitting needle, blend it into the body. Cut two 1" (25 mm) squares from your sheet. Crosscut them to make four triangles. Gently place the four triangles around the rim and blend them in with your knitting needle. Pinch the edges of the four triangles so the edges taper and are not flat where you cut them. Gently curl the edges in a bit, like petals on a rose.

6 DETAILING THE BOTTOM RING

Cut another piece ½" by 2" (13 mm x 51 mm) from your sheet, and roll it between your palms into a thin rope approximately ⅛" (3 mm) thick. Cut off the pointed ends ¾" (20 mm) in length. Roll the remainder again between your palms and cut off the pointed ends again, so now you have four tapered ends. Gently place them inside the ring as shown and use your knitting needle to blend them in.

7 TEXTURING THE LEGS

Cut six pieces of beading wire approximately 3" (76 mm) in length. Using your fingers, lightly coat the wires with white glue and set them aside to dry. With another piece of wire, a knitting needle, or toothpick, make texture marks around the edges of the legs so they have little folds and wrinkles like carrots. After the glue has dried, carefully poke the wires through each leg, leaving approximately ⅜" (10 mm) protruding from the thicker end.

8 ATTACHING THE LEGS

Insert the leg wire and press the top of the leg onto the lower part of the main body. Make another long thin rope of clay and wrap it around where the leg joins the body. Using your knitting needle, blend the rope into the leg and body, smoothing it out until the joint lines disappear. Attach the second leg in the same way opposite the first. Now comes the tricky part. Holding the body in front of you, mark two more points with the tip of your knitting needle equally divided where the other two legs will go on both sides. Now, fill in the remaining four legs, two on each side, and clip off the ends of the wires protruding from the tips of the feet. Turn your alien right side up and set it down so it stands on a tabletop. Gently bend and move the legs until your creature looks straight.

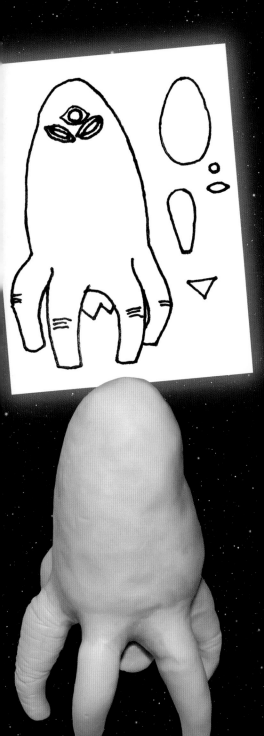

9 MAKING THE EYES

From a variety pack of colored clay, roll a piece of red clay into a rope about $^3/_{16}$" (5 mm) thick and cut off three pieces approximately $^3/_{16}$" (5 mm) long. Roll two of these between the palms of your hands into double-pointed egg shapes. Roll the third piece into a round ball. Place all three into a glass pan and bake for ½ hour. When they are completely cooled, position them onto the head of your alien and push them down into the soft clay.

10 FINISHING THE EYES

Now we're going to make eyelids. Once again, roll a long rope of clay between the palms of your hands and place two pieces around each eye. With your toothpick, blend all the edges in so they form top and bottom eyelids. Now go back and retexture the body of your alien as well as the legs. You can drag a toothpick or comb across the body to make wrinkles. Carefully place your alien on a folded up dish towel or old sock, making certain you don't bend the legs. Place it in the oven and bake at 275°F (135°C) for one hour. When the baking time is up, turn the oven off and let your creature cool so it doesn't break or crack.

11 PAINTING THE ALIEN

There are many different techniques to painting clay sculpture. You can make a very thin wash of acrylic paint and slowly build up colored layers, waiting for each coat to dry before applying the next. It is a good idea to bake up a couple of scrap pieces of clay to experiment on before painting your sculpture. For this alien, I applied a solid coat of black. After it dried, I painted turquoise stripes with a small brush. Lastly, using a stiff brush dipped in the tiniest amount of titanium white, I lightly dry-brushed the red eyeballs and added blue pupils with the tiniest of brushes.

That is a great question! As director of science information at the Harvard-Smithsonian Center for Astrophysics in Cambridge, Massachusetts, it is my job to publicize and create images for newly discovered exoplanets, track discoveries reported by other organizations including NASA, and attend international science conferences. So, writing an exciting new book like this was a natural for me.

To help create the planets profiled in this book—each modeled after real planet discoveries, but expanded into a fully imagined world—I spent months reading scientific papers posted in journals online and meeting with experts in the field. Dr. Lisa Kaltenegger, exobiology expert from the Max Planck Institute in Germany, assisted me in narrowing down the parameters for these eight alien worlds. We talked for hours about how much gravity each world would have, what orbit it would be in, how big it might be. I also consulted with Dr. Ray Jayawardhana, Canada Research Chair in Observational Astrophysics at the University of Toronto, who helped me narrow down the climate conditions on these worlds. For the biological aspects and possibilities of life, I consulted with Dr. Dimitar Sasselov, director of the Origins of Life Initiative at Harvard University; E. O. Wilson, professor of biology at Harvard University;

Freeman Dyson, retired professor of theoretical physics at Princeton University; and Andrew Knoll, professor of natural history at Harvard University. And, of course, I read every new book written by the top scientists in the field, including James Kasting, Peter Ward, Ray Jayawardhana, Dimitar Sasselov, Sara Seager, Neil Comins, Freeman Dyson, Ray Villard, and Joel Garreau.

But how did I make these aliens? In my art studio, I used a combination of techniques to make these creatures come to life. Some were glued together out of styrene plastic. Some were sculpted out of polymer clay. Then they were digitally photographed and detailed using a computer program called Photoshop. It took hours to digitally add skin textures, colors, alien eyes, etc. Next, I digitally painted the backgrounds and added the aliens to them, much like they do in Hollywood movies.

What I accomplished was a book that applies the best science we have to a largely unknown canvas—the realm beyond our solar system. This process of scientifically based speculation created imagined realms that could actually exist. As odd as some of these alien environments and the life-forms that inhabit them look, I am certain even stranger things exist out there! This is your passport to the miracles of life in the universe!

David Aguilar in his studio

RESOURCES

EXOPLANET INTERACTIVE WEBSITES

Alien Earths
www.alienearths.org/index.php

Deep Space Activities: Exoplanets
www.roe.ac.uk/vc/education/secondary/
exoplanets.html

Habitable Zone Gallery
web.ipac.caltech.edu/staff/skane/hzgallery/
index.html

Harvard MicroObservatory
mo-www.cfa.harvard.edu/MicroObservatory

Kepler Space Mission
kepler.nasa.gov
kepler.nasa.gov/education/activities

**Las Cumbres Observatory—Agent
Exoplanet**
lcogt.net/education/agentexoplanet

**MicroObservatory Robotic Telescope
Network**
mo-www.cfa.harvard.edu/MicroObservatory

NASA PlanetQuest
exep.jpl.nasa.gov/aye

NASA Quest for Planets
missionscience.nasa.gov/nasascience/
quest_for_exoplanets.html

neoK12 Educational Videos
www.neok12.com/Exoplanets.htm

Royal Observatory Greenwich
www.rmg.co.uk/royal-observatory

7 Amazing Exoplanets (Interactive)
www.scientificamerican.com/article
.cfm?id=7-amazing-exoplanets-interactive

EXOPLANET NEWS WEB SOURCES

www.astronomy.com
www.badastronomy.com/index.html
www.cfa.harvard.edu/news/press.html
news.discovery.com/space/alien-life
-exoplanets
www.skyandtelescope.com
www.space.com

GREAT ASTRONOMY WEBSITES

Astronomical Society of the Pacific
astrosociety.org/about-us
www.astrosociety.org/astroshop

Astronomy Picture of the Day
apod.nasa.gov/apod/astropix.html

Cool Cosmos
coolcosmos.ipac.caltech.edu

Night Sky Network
nightsky.jpl.nasa.gov/club-map.cfm

GREAT YOUTUBE EXOPLANET SITES

How Exoplanets Are Identified
PART 1
www.youtube.com/watch?v=ewJ-YGBaAlE
PART 2
www.youtube.com/
watch?v=nO9tdUROMhg

Size of Things in the Universe
www.youtube.com/
watch?v=HEheh1BH34Q

10 Most Amazing Exoplanets
www.youtube.com/watch?v=fJUmptj09GY

**Welcome to the Universe: The Size of
Things**
www.youtube.com/watch?v=N_RqlTi6wGY

GREAT BOOKS FOR FURTHER STUDY

Barlowe's Guide to Extraterrestrials,
Wayne Douglas Barlowe, Workman Publishing, 1979.

Bird Sense: What It's Like To Be A Bird,
Tim Birkhead, Walker & Company, 2012.

*Creating Life-Like Animals in Polymer
Clay,* Katherine Dewey, North Light
Books, 2000.

Faraway Worlds, Paul Halpern, Charles-
bridge Publishing, 2004.

Infinite Worlds, Ray Villard and Lynette R.
Cook, University of California Press, 2005.

A Natural History of the Senses, Diane
Ackerman, Random House, 1990.

Other Senses, Other Worlds, Doris &
David Jonas, Stein & Day Publishers, 1976.

The Science of Aliens, Clifford Pickover,
Basic Books, 1998.

What a Plant Knows, Daniel Chamovitz,
Scientific American, 2012.

CHECK OUT MY AUTHOR PAGES AT:

www.aspenskies.com
www.davidaguilar.org

ASTRONOMERS Scientists who study the dimensions, positions, and motions of the universe and the objects in it, such as stars, planets, nebulae, and galaxies.

ATMOSPHERE The gases and "air" surrounding a celestial body, held in place by that celestial body's gravitational field.

AURORA An atmospheric phenomenon in the polar regions of Earth that appears as vivid bands of light in the sky. This phenomenon is caused by collisions between electrically charged particles from the sun's solar wind smashing into Earth's upper atmospheric gases. These collisions release photons, or particles of light.

BIOLUMINESCENT Living organisms emitting light as a result of an organic chemical reaction.

CHLOROPHYLL A green pigment found in plants, and some algae and bacteria, that is essential to photosynthesis—the production of energy from light.

ELECTROLYTE A solution or molten substance that conducts electricity by way of electrically charged particles called ions.

EXOPLANETS Planets that orbit a star in a solar system other than ours. Our solar system includes the sun and the planets that orbit it, including Mercury, Venus, Earth, Mars, Jupiter, Saturn, Uranus, Neptune, and the dwarf planets (Eris, Pluto, and Ceres), and even some asteroids and comets.

FOLIAGE The abundance or presence of leaves, flowers, and branches.

GAMMA RAYS Photons of penetrating electromagnetic radiation with wavelengths shorter than about one-tenth of a nanometer.

GRAVITY The force that pulls matter toward the center of the Earth or any large celestial mass.

HABITABLE ZONE Sometimes called the "Goldilocks zone," this is the specific region around a star where it is theoretically possible for a planet to have sufficient atmospheric pressure to maintain liquid water on its surface.

HEXAPOD An animal with six feet.

ICE AGES Cold periods in Earth's history characterized by extensive glaciation in the Northern Hemisphere. The most recent ice age ended about 10,000 years ago. During this last ice age, great sheets of ice up to 2 miles (3 km) thick covered most of Greenland, Canada, and the northern United States, as well as northern Europe and Russia.

INFRARED The part of the electromagnetic spectrum with a longer wavelength than light but a shorter wavelength than radio waves. These wavelengths are invisible to the naked eye.

LIGHT-YEAR The distance light travels in a vacuum in one year. It equals 5,878,625,373,184 miles (9,460,730,472,581 km). It is used as a measurement for distance in space.

RADIAL SYMMETRY The body structure of an organism where a vertical cut through the center of the organism in any two or more places would result in two halves that are mirror images of each other. Think of a wheel, a flower, or a sea urchin.

SOLAR FLARE A sudden, violent explosion of energy that occurs in the sun's atmosphere near a sunspot.

SONAR The emission of sound waves to detect the position of objects. Examples of animals that use sonar are dolphins, whales, and bats.

No planet outside our solar system has a proper name. Instead, exoplanets are cataloged by the sky survey that found them, the number assigned to the star in the survey, and a letter of the alphabet indicating in what order they orbit the star. For example, a planet found with the OGLE (Optical Gravitational Lensing Experiment) might be known as OGLE-45c. This means it is the 45th star in the survey and the planet is the second farthest away from the star. The letter "a" counts as the star. If our sun were star #65 on the OGLE list, Earth would be listed as OGLE-65d. Exciting, huh? Since all the planets in our solar system are named after Greek gods, I mostly stuck with that idea for my exoplanets, even though I was tempted to name one of them "Wayne."

I decided to give my planets real names. Many exoplanets known today do resemble my planets, only mine have names you can remember.

SILURIANA was named after the Silurian geological period on Earth, when life in the oceans was just beginning to move onto land. This started about 443 million years ago. Siluriana is younger than Earth.

YELRIHS-57e is a made-up survey name and the planet is the fourth planet from the star, just like Mars.

CHAOS is the Greek name for the place of disorder . . . exactly what is happening on this planet!

MOROS is the Greek god of doom and fate. It fits. Planet Moros is slowly dying.

VENERA was the name the Soviet Union gave to their Venus landers. "Venera" means Venus.

ARCLANDIA is a made-up name. I always liked the symphony *Finlandia*, so I joined "Arc" from arctic and "landia," a Finnish word for land, together.

HYPNOS is the Greek word for sleep. We use it in the word "hypnotize" which means sleeping while awake.

CHRONOS was the Greek Father of Time. The artificial life on this planet is going to exist for a very long time.

INDEX

**Published by the
National Geographic Society**

John M. Fahey,
*Chairman of the Board and Chief
Executive Officer*

Declan Moore,
*Executive Vice President;
President, Publishing and Travel*

Melina Gerosa Bellows,
*Executive Vice President;
Chief Creative Officer, Books, Kids,
and Family*

Prepared by the Book Division

Hector Sierra,
*Senior Vice President and
General Manager*

Nancy Laties Feresten,
*Senior Vice President,
Kids Publishing and Media*

Jay Sumner,
*Director of Photography,
Children's Publishing*

Jennifer Emmett,
*Vice President, Editorial Director,
Children's Books*

Eva Absher-Schantz,
*Design Director, Kids Publishing
and Media*

R. Gary Colbert,
Production Director

Jennifer A. Thornton,
Director of Managing Editorial

Staff for This Book

Jennifer Emmett,
Project Editor

David M. Seager,
Art Director

Lori Epstein,
Senior Photo Editor

Ariane Szu-Tu,
Editorial Assistant

Callie Broaddus,
Design Production Assistant

Hillary Moloney,
Associate Photo Editor

Grace Hill,
Associate Managing Editor

Joan Gossett,
Production Editor

Lewis R. Bassford,
Production Manager

Susan Borke,
Legal and Business Affairs

Production Services

Phillip L. Schlosser,
Senior Vice President

Chris Brown, *Vice President,
NG Book Manufacturing*

George Bounelis, *Vice President,
Production Services*

Nicole Elliott, *Manager*

Rachel Faulise, *Manager*

Robert L. Barr, *Manager*

*I would like to thank Dr. Dimitar Sasselov, director of the Harvard Origins of
Life Initiative, and Dr. Lisa Kaltenegger, exobiology expert at the Max Planck
Institute, for their expertise and help with these alien worlds.*

*I dedicate this book to Shirley, Queen of the Asteroids, whom I could not
love more; visionary and friend David M. Seager, NGS art director
extraordinaire; Arthur C. Clarke; Wayne Douglas Barlowe; and
Gort "Klatu-Barrada-Nikto!" D.A.*

Illustration Credits

All artwork by David Aguilar unless otherwise noted below:
Shutterstock: p 16: whale shark, macaw, panda; p 17: butterfly, snake,
bumble bee, bat, insects flower, fly, starfish, worm; p 69: wire cutters, glue,
rolling pin, needle, clay, foil, knife, paint, ruler, toothpicks, paintbrushes, wire

The National Geographic Society is one of the world's largest nonprofit
scientific and educational organizations. Founded in 1888 to "increase and
diffuse geographic knowledge," the Society's mission is to inspire people
to care about the planet. It reaches more than 400 million
people worldwide each month through its official journal, *National
Geographic*, and other magazines; National Geographic Channel;
television documentaries; music; radio; films; books; DVDs; maps;
exhibitions; live events; school publishing programs; interactive media;
and merchandise. National Geographic has funded more than 10,000
scientific research, conservation, and exploration projects and supports
an education program promoting geographic literacy.

For more information, please visit www.nationalgeographic.com, call
1-800-NGS LINE (647-5463), or write to the following address:

National Geographic Society
1145 17th Street N.W.
Washington, D.C. 20036-4688 U.S.A.

Visit us online at nationalgeographic.com/books

For librarians and teachers: ngchildrensbooks.org

More for kids from National Geographic: kids.nationalgeographic.com

For information about special discounts for bulk purchases, please contact
National Geographic Books Special Sales: ngspecsales@ngs.org

For rights or permissions inquiries, please contact National Geographic
Books Subsidiary Rights: ngbookrights@ngs.org

Trade Hardcover ISBN: 978-1-4263-1110-9
Reinforced Library ISBN: 978-1-4263-1111-6

Printed in China
13/RRDS/1